(M)OTHER

Sanita Fejzić
Alisa Arsenault

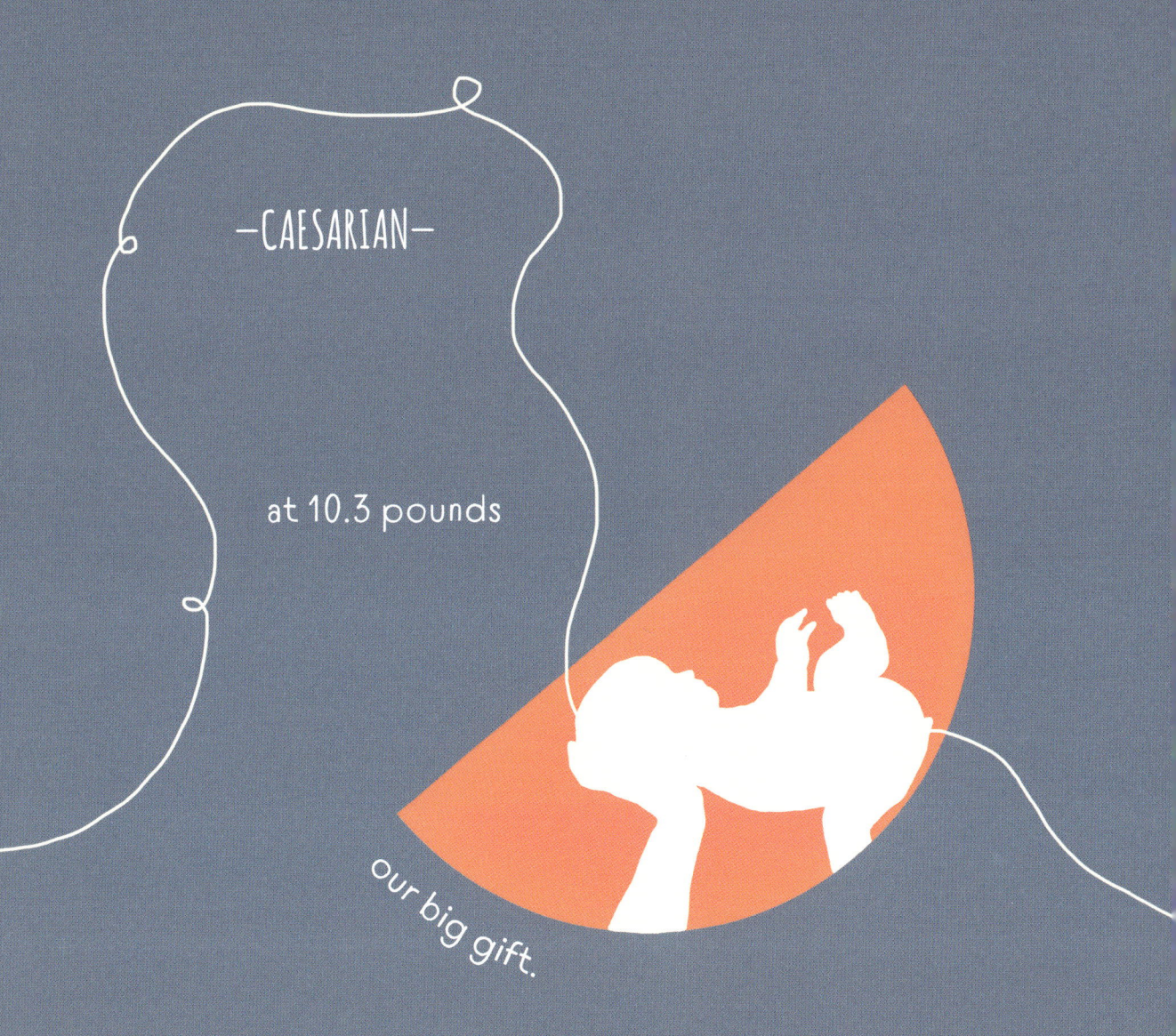

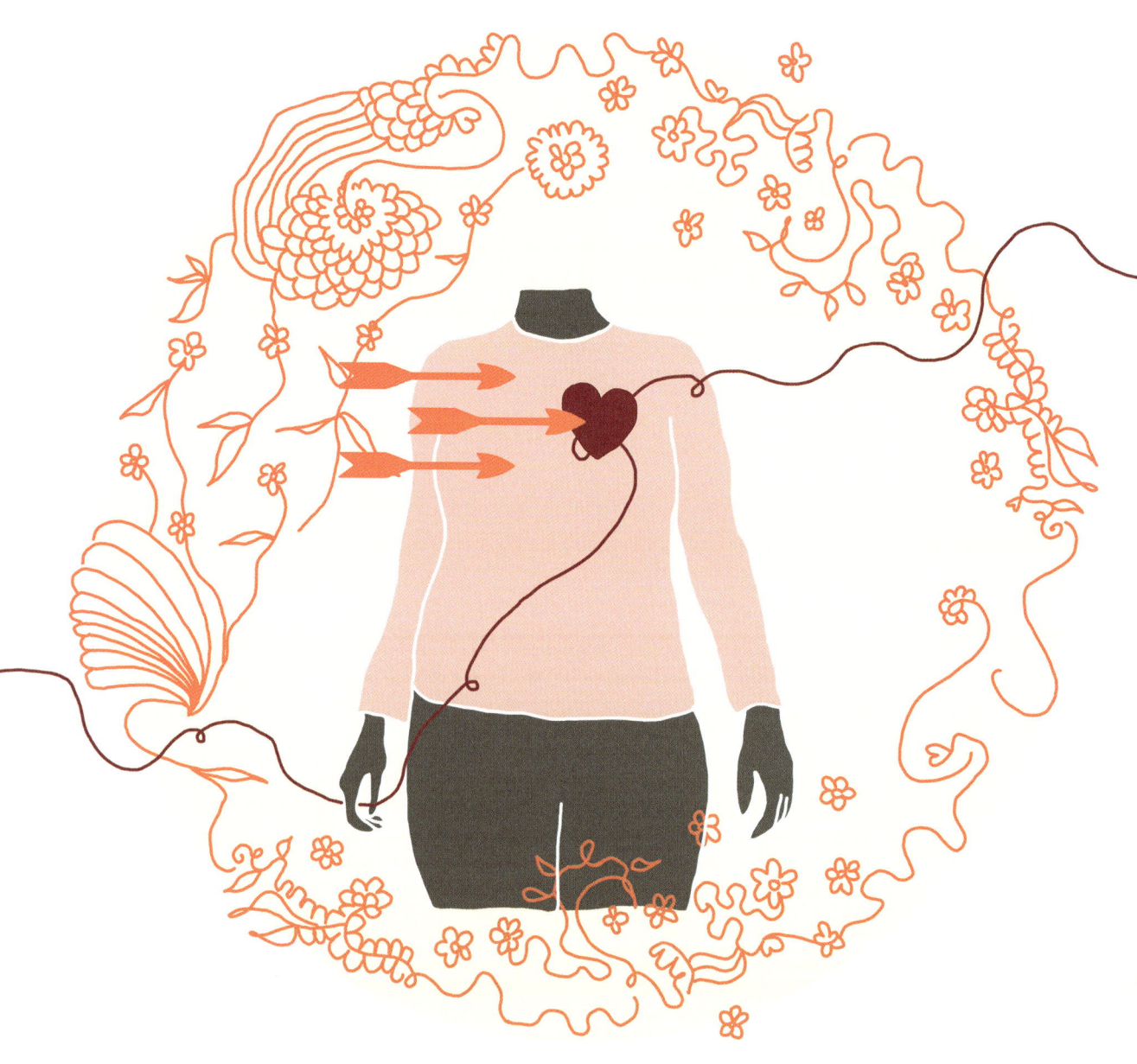

Their words hit me in the chest:

"HA! HA! PA! PA! PA!"

They darted by:

"PA! PAPA!"

When I asked the teacher to talk to them she said, "They're just children."

SO ARE YOU, MY SON.

The one that's learning to be light
to laugh when others look for a father

like that time I made you giggle at Toys R Us
holding up a mask of Padmé Amidala to my face

exhaling in a deeply performative tone:

"I AM YOUR (M)OTHER."

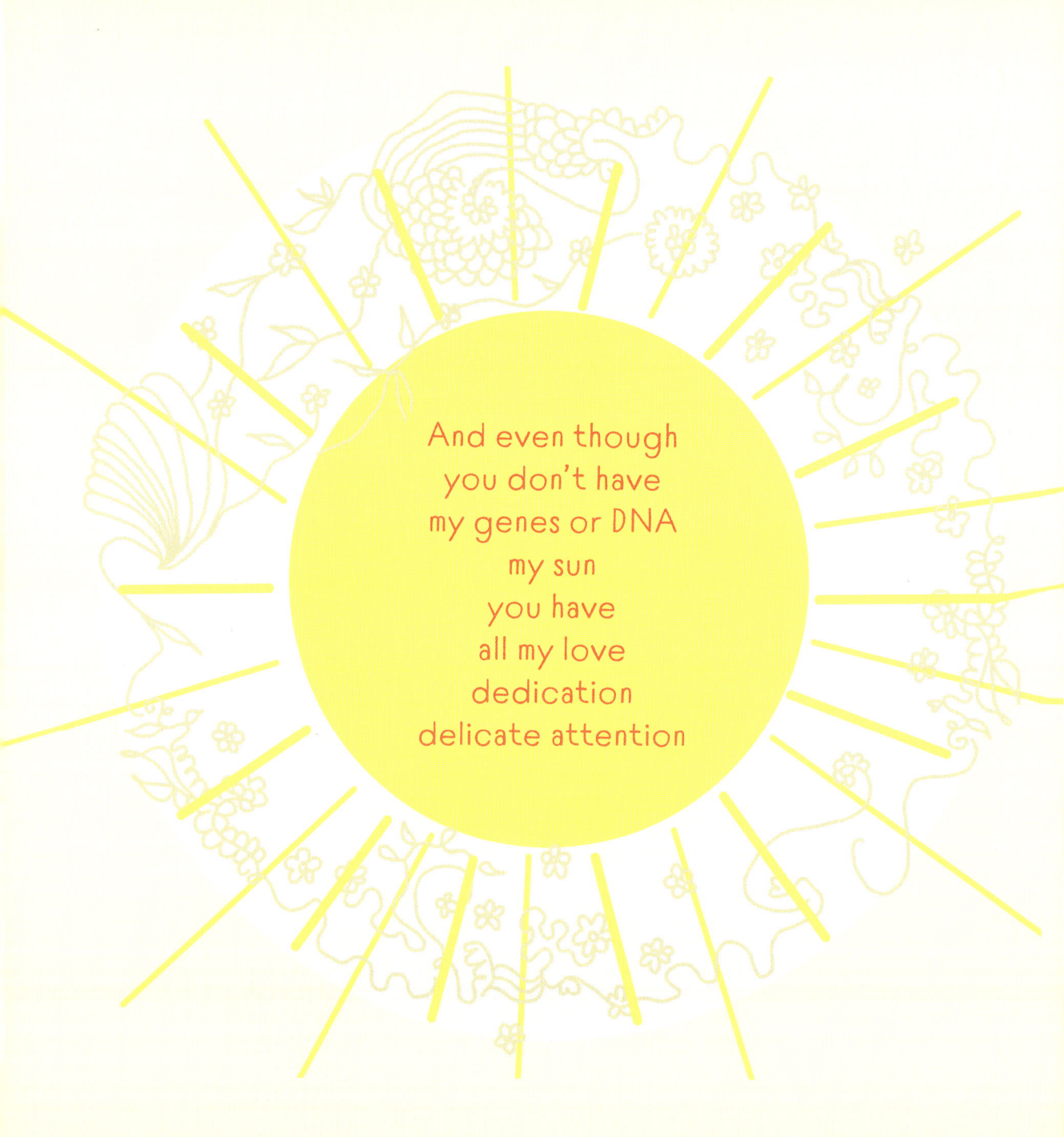

Title: (M)other
Author: Sanita Fejzić
Illustrations: Alisa Arsenault
Editing: Jo-Ann Elder, Réjean Ouellette
Graphic Design: Atelier 46
Projects Manager: Léonore Bailhache
Literary Director: Marie Cadieux

ISBN 978-2-89750-185-3
ISBN (PDF) 978-2-89750-186-0
ISBN ePUB 978-2-89750-187-7

Copyright © 2019 Bouton d'or Acadie
Library and Archives Canada
Printed in Canada by Transcontinental

All rights of reproduction, adaptation
and translation reserved for all countries.

For its publishing activities,
Bouton d'or Acadie acknowledges
the financial support of:

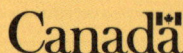 

Distributed in French by Prologue
Phone: (450) 434-0306 / 1 800 363-2864
Fax: (450) 434-2627 / 1 800 361-8088
Email: prologue@prologue.ca

Distributed by Nimbus Publishing
P.O. Box 9166, Halifax, NS B3K 5M8
Phone: 1-800-646-2879
Fax: 902-455-5440
Email: customerservice@nimbus.ca

© Bouton d'or Acadie inc.
P.O. Box 575, Moncton, NB E1C 8L9, Canada
Phone: (506) 382-1367
Email: info@boutondoracadie.com

 This book is also available
in eBook format

 Bouton d'or Acadie is a member
of the Regroupement des éditeurs
franco-canadiens.

Created in Acadie. Printed in Canada.
www.boutondoracadie.com